PRAISE FOR
MAGNIFICENT MAJESTIC MONO LAKE

Magnificent Majestic Mono Lake is a rich read for anyone who enjoys nature study. The book is clear and freshly researched, and the nature stories within will teach you new things about our wild neighbors and in some cases help you reconsider what you thought you knew! I was delighted to learn how pikas survive the heat near Mono Lake – their hidden cooling system is surprising! The illustrations and design match the color palette of the region and beautifully support the book – you want to pick it up and turn the pages. This lovely book is a welcome resource for nature lovers and stewards of wild places.

John Muir Laws – Author of *The Laws Field Guide to the Sierra Nevada* **and** *The Laws Guide to Nature Drawing and Journaling*

Beautifully illustrated and expertly written, this marvelous book tells the story of Mono Lake's unique ecosystem and remarkable water history. Informative profiles of the birds, wildlife, and plants of the area include discussion of the impacts of water diversions, highlighting the important role we all play in protecting special places like Mono Lake!

Geoffrey McQuilkin – Executive Director, Mono Lake Committee

Magnificent Majestic Mono Lake is a colorfully illustrated and fascinating dive into the nature of Mono Lake. Andrew and Harriet Smith go beyond the unique ecosystem of the lake itself to reveal stories of birds, mammals, insects, reptiles, amphibians and plants in the surrounding watershed. I learned so many new facts about a place where I worked as a ranger for 20 years, and have called home for 40 years. What a magnificent, majestic way to learn about amazing Mono Lake.

David Carle – Author of *Traveling the 38th Parallel – A Waterline Around the World* **and** *Mono Lake Viewpoint*

Magnificent Majestic Mono Lake is a beautiful book about a wonderful region, carefully researched and delightfully portrayed, ideal as an introduction to the geology, hydrology, flora, fauna, and ecology. The Smiths provide a model visitor's guide — pointing out what to look for and why each actor in the basin's complicated system matters. At the same time, the book delivers a sobering message, that such ecosystems are always at risk and require continuing care.

Michael P. Cohen — Author of *Granite and Grace: Seeking the Heart of Yosemite* **and** *A Garden of Bristlecones: Tales of Change in the Great Basin*

Magnificent Majestic Mono Lake tells the intriguing history of the formation of Mono Lake, the lake's dynamics, and the past, present, and future threats to this unique ecosystem. Engaging stories about the ecosystem's birds, bunnies, bugs, and reptiles are accompanied by vivid full-page color illustrations. The contents will surprise both newcomers and devoted visitors to this region — like the description of ancient dragonflies with two-foot wingspans and now-extinct cheetahs chasing pronghorns along the shore of Mono Lake.

Deanna Dulen — First Director of the Mono Basin Scenic Area Visitor Center and former Superintendent of Devil's Postpile National Monument

MAGNIFICENT MAJESTIC
MONO LAKE

Andrew Smith & Harriet Smith
Illustration: Roni Alexander

MAGNIFICENT MAJESTIC MONO LAKE

Subjects: Natural History, Conservation, Mono Lake

ISBN 978-1-954000-30-8 (Paperback)

Authors: Andrew Smith and Harriet Smith

Illustrations: Roni Alexander

Published 2022, by Publish Authority

PublishAuthority.com

Printed in the United States of America

TABLE OF CONTENTS

WHAT'S SO SPECIAL ABOUT MONO LAKE

A lake larger than the city of San Francisco and saltier than any ocean. Limestone towers jutting out of the water like alien beings. Endless vistas of blue skies and high desert scrubland dotted with dormant volcanoes and sagebrush. This is California's Mono Lake and the surrounding Mono Basin, a strange and extraordinary ecosystem.

Like other salt lakes, fresh water flows into but not out of Mono Lake, so water is trapped in a gigantic basin. As liquid evaporates from a salt lake, the dissolved chemicals in the water remain, making the water even saltier and more alkaline. To make up for water lost by evaporation, salt lakes need regular infusions of fresh water from feeder streams. This is especially important in dry desert environments, like the Great Basin Desert surrounding Mono Lake. But water in the desert is so scarce that it is often diverted from feeder streams to meet the needs of humans. The result? The lake level drops, salinity and alkalinity increase, the water becomes lethal to its plant and animal inhabitants, and the entire ecosystem collapses. At the point when the lake has completely evaporated, all that remains is toxic alkaline dust.

Most salt lakes in the world, like the Aral Sea, have already dried up or are at high risk of drying because less water enters the lake than is lost through evaporation or diversion. Mono Lake, on the other hand, remains healthy, supports a vibrant ecosystem, and sustains an active ecotourism industry.

Why is Mono Lake thriving while other salt lakes are drying up? One reason is water—unlike most other salt lakes, Mono Lake continues to receive fresh water from its feeder streams. Mono Lake abuts the eastern flank of the Sierra Nevada Mountains, and water from melting winter snows delivered by five streams replenishes the lake with pristine water from the High Sierra.

Perhaps the most important reason that Mono Lake continues to thrive is that its watershed is now protected by law, thanks to massive and ongoing efforts by citizen activists, students, and scientists to conserve this extraordinary ecosystem. As a result of a long battle between conservationists and the Los Angeles Department of Water and Power, which continues to this day, the state of California in 1994 established a plan for the management of Mono Lake which mandated that enough water be released into the lake from feeder streams to insure a healthy home for all its inhabitants.

In the pages ahead you will learn about the erupting volcanoes which have left their imprint on Mono Lake, the lake's simple ecosystem that provides food for millions of breeding and migrating birds, and some of the plants and animals that inhabit the Mono Basin. Finally, you will learn about ongoing threats to Mono Lake and its basin, and what you can do to help protect this magical place.

HOW IT ALL BEGAN

A fracturing of the earth three-to-four million years ago created a huge geographic area, called the Basin and Range, with no connection to the ocean. Without an outlet to the sea, all precipitation drains internally—it either evaporates, seeps underground, or fills empty basins, creating lakes in an otherwise high, dry desert. Mono Lake, sitting in the Mono Basin, became a lake in just this way.

Lakes with no outlet, like Mono Lake, typically become salt lakes. When lake levels drop in years of low precipitation, water evaporation increases the concentration of salt. In years with heavy precipitation, the opposite occurs—lake level rises and salt concentration decreases.

Mono Lake today is the end result of many ice ages, its depth rising and falling as huge glaciers melted, dried up, and then repeated the cycle. Although Mono Lake appears vast, it is actually only a fraction of its former size, when it was called Lake Russell. Thousands of years ago, it was eight hundred feet deep, twenty-eight miles long, and eighteen miles wide. Today it is 160 feet deep at the deepest and covers only about half of its former geographic area.

Compared to other lakes in North America, Mono Lake is ancient—it has been a living lake for over 760,000 years. Unlike many other salt lakes, like Owens Lake in California, Mono Lake has never dried out. It supports an ecosystem of trillions of plants and animals, most of which are smaller than a fingernail, but which feed millions of breeding and migrating birds every year.

Ice ages and earth fractures are only part of the creation story of Mono Lake. Volcanoes, fresh water springs, and the feisty young Sierra Nevada mountain range tell the rest of the story.

WHERE THE WATER COMES FROM

Because Mono Lake is close to the Sierra Nevada Mountains, it benefits from rushing streams flush with snowmelt that empty into it every spring. Five feeder streams replenish Mono Lake with fresh water, preventing the lake from becoming too salty as water evaporates during the year. Without these feeder streams, Mono Lake would not exist.

Rush Creek, Lee Vining Creek, and Mill Creek all empty into the western side of Mono Lake from the Sierra. Walker and Parker Creeks join Rush Creek, delivering a blast of fresh water into the lake every spring.

It is easy to locate these creeks in the surrounding sea of sagebrush—look for the ribbons of green winding through the desert vegetation from the mountains to the lake. Vegetation on these stream banks looks nothing like the

WALKER

PARKER

RUSH

plant communities growing nearby. These "riparian" areas are thick with quaking aspen, black cottonwood, and coyote willow, interspersed with thickets of buffalo berry and mountain rose.

The riparian forest provides different insect and plant foods from those found in the arid, upland Mono Basin, and supports a wide variety of bird, reptile, and amphibian species that couldn't survive in the markedly different plant community a few feet away. Fish inhabit some of the feeder streams but don't venture beyond the point where the streams empty into the lake because they would be unable to survive the water's high salt and alkaline content.

The diversion of Mono Lake feeder streams in the early 1940s to provide water for the City of Los Angeles almost destroyed Mono Lake. If the diversion hadn't been halted as a result of the efforts of a plucky band of activists determined to protect this unique ecosystem, all that would remain of the lake would be a dry, toxic, salt playa.

MILL

LEE VINING

A LANDSCAPE OF VOLCANOES

Driving north toward Mono Lake on Highway 395, volcanoes surround us. West of the highway are the Inyo Craters and east of it are the Mono Craters, the youngest mountain chain in North America. The Mono Craters began erupting around forty thousand years ago and will undoubtedly erupt again sometime in the future. The youngest of the Mono Craters, Panum Crater, lies within a mile of Mono Lake and last erupted six hundred years ago.

What lies underneath volcanoes explains why they erupt—chambers of liquid, molten rock, called magma. Gasses trapped within the magma are released when pressure builds, as when groundwater vaporizes in the presence of the fiery hot magma. The magma then explodes up to the surface through fissures from the magma chamber, creating an explosion pit above ground. Magma that reaches the surface, called lava, eventually covers and seals the fissure, and the eruption ceases. What remains after the fissure is sealed is a steep, exposed dome of dried lava covered with thick gray ash. From below, the ash covering the Mono Craters looks smooth and velvety, but if you try to walk on it, you will sink to your knees in this "rhyolite sand," and make forward progress only with Herculean effort.

Sitting in Mono Lake are two large islands that were both produced by volcanic eruptions. The large white island, "Paoha," is a mere youngster that emerged a little over three hundred years ago and consists mostly of white lake-bottom mud. The people native to the Mono Basin, the Mono Lake Kutzadika'a Tribe, named Paoha for tiny spirits with long wavy hair that they visualized in the clouds of vapor that rose from the lake. The older black island, "Negit," emerged 1600 years ago. Negit may be the native word for "goose" or "gull," but no one knows for sure. The presence of hot springs and steam vents beneath these dormant volcanoes are a sure sign that they too will erupt again.

Black Point, on the northwest shore of the lake, erupted underwater over thirteen thousand years ago, when Mono Lake was eight hundred feet deep. Black Point remained totally submerged until the lake level dropped low enough to expose its broad, dark dome. At the top of the dome are fissures, some several feet wide and a hundred feet deep, through which the magma burst at the time of the last eruption.

A CHEMICAL SEA

Because Mono Lake has no outlet and sits in a basin dotted with volcanoes, the chemical composition of its water is determined by the presence of igneous (once molten) rock, salts from surrounding desert soils, and sulfates from both volcanic rocks and Sierra Nevada granite. Because some water slowly travels underground to reach the lake, salts and other minerals from volcanic rock and calcium from the soil have time to dissolve into the water before it percolates up into the lake.

Mono Lake water is three times saltier and eighty times more alkaline than the ocean. The alkalinity of the water makes the water taste bitter and feel slippery, like soap suds. In *Roughing It*, Mark Twain hilariously described the joy of washing his clothes in Mono Lake this way: "Its sluggish waters are so strong with alkali that if you only dip the most hopelessly soiled garment into them once or twice, and wringing it out, will be found as clean as if it had been through the ablest of washerwoman's hands."

The heaviness of Mono Lake water makes it reflective, like a mirror. Whenever you visit the lake, depending on time of day, local weather, or season, its color will be a spectacularly different shade of blue. Ice blue, turquoise, dark teal, midnight blue, and in the winter, a deep murky green reflect the many moods of Mono Lake and make each visit different from the last.

TOWERS OF LIMESTONE

The attention of a first-time visitor to Mono Lake is instantly captured by the limestone towers, or tufa, jutting out of the lake. Although tufa is found in other salt lakes, nowhere else does it grow into the fantastical formations unique to Mono Lake.

These tall limestone spires form when alkaline Mono Lake water and fresh spring water come into contact. Cool spring water, embedded in sand underneath the lake bed, is essential for the creation of tufa. Calcium in spring water combines with carbonate salts in lake water to create stunning limestone formations, normally hidden from view beneath the lake's surface.

Like stalagmites and stalactites found in caves, tufa is made of calcium carbonate. It has a spongelike interior and a hard exterior. About an inch of tufa forms underwater every day and attaches to the mass of limestone at the point where spring water comes into contact with lake water. Tufa grows along the pathway of the bubbling fresh water as it rises through faults in the lake bottom.

So, how do we explain the spires of tufa protruding from the water and dotting the dry land close to the shoreline? Because tufa forms only under water, it can't attach to tufa that is above the surface. When Mono Lake's level drops to the point that tufa is no longer submerged, the exposed tufa simply stops growing. Tufa pillars stranded on land reveal how much depth the lake has lost since the tufa was last under water. David Gaines poetically described these relics as "Marooned on shore by receding waters, they seem like the bones of a shrinking lake."

We are asked not to climb on exposed tufa because when the exterior is broken, the structure crumbles. Islands of tufa on land, whether revealing their multiple pastel hues in summer or powdered with winter snow, add to the splendor of Mono Lake. And they are put to good use by nesting birds like violet-green swallows, rock wrens, and Say's phoebes, just to name a few.

ALKALI FLIES, BRINE SHRIMP, AND ALGAE—OH MY!

It is hard to imagine that an ecosystem consisting primarily of three species (with some bacteria thrown in) could produce enough food to feed millions of birds every year. Ensuring the health of these three species—alkali flies, brine shrimp, and algae—is vital, because the loss of any of them would spell the collapse of the entire ecosystem.

The easiest to observe of these primary species are alkali flies, which encircle the lake at the water's edge in the millions during summer, like a thick black ribbon. The flies spend most of their time busily foraging on algae that has floated ashore. When we disturb them by stepping into their midst, they scatter and then immediately return to the shoreline, never deigning to land on, much less pester, us humans.

Alkali flies can crawl on tufa under water, stay submerged indefinitely by breathing air trapped in their body hair, and osmoregulate by pumping salt and minerals out of their bodies. They are prolific, high in fat content, and apparently taste pretty good, making a nutritious meal for the migrating and breeding birds that ingest them by the millions each year. The Paiute Tribe native to the area around Mono Lake, the Kutzadika'a, named themselves after the pupae of alkali flies (Kutzadika'a means "eater of brine flies") because the tribe's way of life depended on eating and trading the "kutsavi" pupae they harvested.

Brine shrimp are thumbnail-sized filter-feeding invertebrates that inhabit Mono Lake by the trillions. They look like filmy white feathers in the water, but their color actually ranges from ocher to turquoise. Like alkali flies, they cope with the water's high salinity and alkalinity by pumping excess salt and minerals from their bodies. Their primary food is algae, but unlike alkali flies, they consume algae floating in open water rather than on the shoreline.

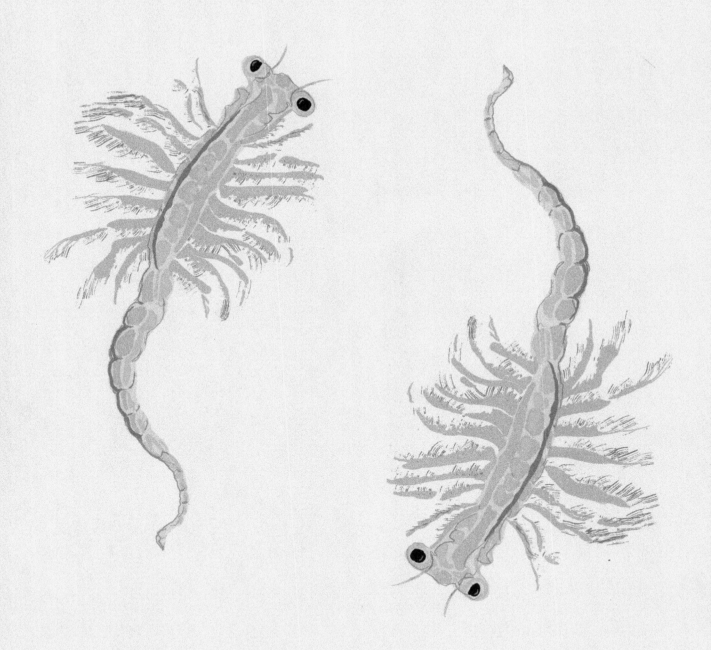

Brine shrimp die in the fall after they release their eggs, which fall to the bottom of the lake. The eggs survive the winter by lying dormant in the lake bed. They hatch sometime between January and April when the water warms and there is plenty of algae to eat. It isn't long before migrating birds stop on the way to their breeding grounds to rest and fatten up on brine shrimp at the Mono Lake oasis.

The most important food source in Mono Lake is one not easily seen by the naked eye, much less by people visiting the lake. Algae is the primary food of Mono Lake alkali flies and brine shrimp. The life cycle and abundance of algae in Mono Lake determine the population sizes of both flies and shrimp, and they have a pronounced effect on the color of Mono Lake as well. In the late fall and winter, when last year's brine shrimp have died or been eaten and eggs have not yet hatched, thick algal blooms turn the water a deep, murky green. When the brine shrimp hatch in early spring and begin to consume the algae, the murkiness clears and the lake is transformed into a pale, reflective, crystal blue.

Last, but not least, the bacteria that inhabit Mono Lake perform a very important function—they clean up the detritus left by the trillions of animals and microscopic plants that live and die in Mono Lake.

The health and longevity of the Mono Lake ecosystem, of course, depends on the composition of its water. If too much fresh water evaporates or is diverted elsewhere, the remaining water will become too salty and/or too alkaline for even these hardy creatures to survive.

A DEADLY BEACH

Not all of Mono Lake is a wonderland of plants and animals capable of feeding millions of birds each year. On the northeastern shore of Mono Lake, far from the areas attractive to visitors, lies an exposed, barren, salt flat, or "playa." When the wind picks up, as it often does around Mono Lake, it whips the alkali salts on the playa into dust storms that are toxic to inhale. This playa is the source of some of the most intense dust storms in the United States, so visitors to Mono Lake avoid visiting this area, for good reason. How did the playa get there?

A playa can form at any salt lake that loses more water than it gains. There are several reasons that a salt lake loses water over time. In drought years, or as a result of human diversion schemes, feeder streams may not deliver enough water to compensate for evaporation. When the water evaporates, it leaves a dry lake bed covered with a thick crust of salts. At the Mono Lake playa, this salty crust contains arsenic and other chemicals considered to be toxic air pollutants, which are potentially carcinogenic to humans when inhaled. In contrast, when feeder streams empty enough fresh water into the lake to sustain its depth, the lake bed remains submerged and the salts dissolve safely into the water. Increased aridity and higher temperatures, both attributable to climate change, also speed up water loss from evaporation and thus increase the size of the playa.

When the City of Los Angeles began diverting the water from feeder streams emptying into Mono Lake in 1941, the lake level began to drop. By 1965, the first of many toxic dust storms on the playa had occurred. The elevation level of Mono Lake today, though higher than its lowest point in 1982, has not yet reached the level necessary to ensure that the lake bed is fully submerged. Until then, the threat of the deadly beach remains.

FUELING UP AT MONO LAKE

Mono Lake was designated as a Western Hemisphere Shorebird Reserve Network site in 1990 because it is an important rest stop for migrating birds. Millions of migratory birds use the Pacific flyway, an aerial highway between North and South America, to travel between their breeding and wintering grounds. Three of the most interesting species stopping at the Mono Lake oasis to fatten up before their grueling migratory flights are Wilson's phalaropes, red-necked phalaropes, and eared grebes.

Wilson's phalaropes arrive in late June, still decked out in their breeding plumage, to prepare for their migration to South America for the winter. In contrast to most polygamous birds, the females, rather than the males, display the snazziest plumage. Females compete fiercely for mates, and their colorful feathers enhance their attractiveness to males. Once courtship is over and the eggs are laid, however, females instantly abandon both their eggs and their mates. Male phalaropes are thus single parents, incubating and rearing chicks with no help from females. So, what does a female do after laying her eggs? She copulates with a second male, lays a second clutch of eggs, and once again, deserts him to parent solo. This type of mating system, called "serial polyandry," is rare in the bird world but is the system of choice among phalaropes.

Up to fourteen percent of the world's population of Wilsons' phalaropes—around eighty thousand birds—stop at Mono Lake to refuel before flying nonstop to their wintering grounds in mid-September. They double their weight by pirouetting in circles on the lake surface, which stirs up their preferred prey, brine shrimp, for an easy meal. After molting into their grayish winter plumage, they are ready to migrate.

Red-necked phalaropes, like all phalaropes, are serially polyandrous, and females actually fight over males for mating rights. Females court potential mates by whirling around them in flight, calling to them, and swimming in circles around them, beckoning them to follow. Once eggs are laid, however, they are just as disinterested in parenthood as their female Wilson's counterparts.

Around sixty thousand red-necked phalaropes stop at Mono Lake every year to ready their bodies for migration, arriving in late July and departing by late September. Summer visitors to Mono Lake can thus feast their eyes on thousands of Wilson's and red-necked phalaropes spinning in the water or twisting and turning in flight, as huge flocks move around the lake.

Last, but surely not least among the migrating visitors to Mono Lake, is the eared grebe, probably the most abundant grebe in the world. Eared grebes are a spectacular sight when they first arrive at Mono Lake in March or April, with their contrasting black and cinnamon breeding plumage, wispy golden facial feathers, and bright red eyes. They arrive at Mono Lake earlier and leave for their wintering grounds later than any other North American migrant, giving them plenty of time to dive for brine shrimp, double their weight, and molt into their dull winter plumage. This is an easy time in the lives of the one-to-two million eared grebes that congregate in huge groups on Mono Lake every fall.

Eared grebes are flightless for nine-to-ten months a year. They literally can't fly while fattening up for their arduous migration of up to 3,700 miles because of the way their bodies change in response to this prolonged period of binge eating—their chest muscles shrink and their digestive organs increase fourfold in size. As the time to migrate approaches, the changes in their bodies reverse—their chest muscles grow and their digestive organs shrink. How eared grebes prepare for migration would be somewhat akin to a human sitting on the couch and gorging on high-protein fatty foods for nearly a year, and then running a marathon.

Perhaps as a result, huge numbers of grebes die during migration. Once the grebes arrive at their migration destination, the changes in their bodies reverse, and they become flightless, once again.

CALIFORNIA GULL

Thousands of California gulls choose the islands in Mono Lake as their breeding grounds every year. In 2019, over eleven thousand nests were counted on the islets near Negit Island. What makes these islands in Mono Lake such a prime spot for breeding? The answer is brine shrimp and alkali flies.

Finding a nutritious, high-protein meal on Mono Lake is a piece of cake—all a gull has to do is open its beak. Trillions of brine shrimp floating in the lake provide a banquet for gulls that requires little effort—like feasting on filet mignon in the bathtub. California gulls also gorge on adult alkali flies at the water's edge, sometimes making a mad dash through the flies with beaks wide open, snapping them up as they go. Larval alkali flies add a tasty source of fat to the diet of Mono Lake's California gulls.

California gull pairs are monogamous during the breeding season and nest on open, bare ground in huge colonies. In theory, eggs and chicks should be safe from ground predators on an island in the middle of a lake. But two huge threats to Mono Lake's breeding California gulls have led to a precipitous decline in the number of nests in recent years. In fact, 2019 marked the lowest number of gull nests in thirty-seven years, down from a high of 32,000 nests in the early 1990s.

The most obvious threat to the California gull rookery is a declining water level. When Mono Lake reached a very low level in 1977, Negit Island, once the preferred site for breeding California gulls at Mono Lake, suddenly became accessible by foot. Coyotes exploited the easy access to the island and gobbled up huge numbers of vulnerable eggs and chicks. The gulls responded by moving their rookery from Negit Island to smaller islets which were still surrounded by water. As of 2021, dropping lake levels have made even those islets vulnerable to coyote predation, so the gulls may again be driven to relocate their breeding sites.

A more recent and insidious threat to California gull breeding colonies at Mono Lake was the sudden rapid growth in 2016 of the non-native invasive plant, five-horn smotherweed, on Negit Island and its islets. Thickets of this waist-high weed quickly covered seventy percent of the bare ground, leaving it unsuitable for nesting.

Luckily for the gulls, conservationists quickly noticed the problem and embraced the challenging task of eliminating this weed from the California gull rookery. Were they successful? See the chapter on invasive species to find out.

OSPREY

Visitors to Mono Lake excitedly point to huge stick nests perched atop spires of tufa that jut above the lake's surface. With their binoculars, they see two large raptors, called ospreys, ministering to their chicks. Because ninety-nine percent of an osprey's diet is fish, why in the world would a pair of ospreys nest in the middle of a lake with no fish?

Apparently, they don't mind commuting. Nesting on tufa in a saline lake has its advantages—neither terrestrial predators, like raccoons, nor aerial predators, like bald eagles, are likely to disturb the nest. With safety covered, all ospreys have to do to feed their young is commute to a nearby freshwater lake, do a bit of fishing, and fly back.

Soaring 30-120 feet above the water, the sharp yellow eyes of an osprey spot a fish swimming beneath the lake's surface. It plunges into the water, grabs its prey, and flies off with its prize still thrashing in its talons. If, like other hawks, ospreys had three toes facing forward and one facing backward, it wouldn't be easy for them to hold onto a slippery, struggling fish in flight. But ospreys have a reversible outer toe which allows them to securely grasp their fish, with two toes facing forward and two facing backward. Average fishing bouts are about twelve minutes long and are successful about a quarter of the time, so an osprey has plenty of time to pick up dinner and head back to the nest to feed its family.

Ospreys migrate to Mono Lake to breed. The first osprey nest at Mono Lake was recorded in the mid-1980s, but it took five years before that first pair managed to successfully produce nestlings. In 2020, there were twelve osprey nests scattered around the lake. Nests are monitored and chicks are banded each year to measure reproductive success. Trying to band rambunctious osprey chicks in a rocking boat is no easy feat, but the opportunity to handle adorable chicks that smell like old fish is an added incentive.

Although ospreys are found worldwide, some populations declined precipitously in the mid-1900s due to the deleterious effects of pesticides. Ospreys have made a roaring comeback since the pesticide DDT was banned in 1972, and the number of nests on Mono Lake has been stable for many years.

RED-WINGED BLACKBIRD

Although the red-winged blackbird is one of the most abundant birds in North America, its behavior isn't mundane in any sense of the word. Male redwings, with their sleek black bodies and fiery red shoulder epaulets, arrive at the saltwater marsh on the northwest shore of Mono Lake in early spring to stake out a prime breeding territory. From a prominent perch, they sing incessantly to attract females willing to build a nest on their territory and mate with them.

The drab brown females arrive at the saltwater marsh a bit later than males and quickly choose a male's territory for nesting. After skulking around in the reeds in search of the best nesting materials, females weave an intricate nest a little above the water line. After copulation occurs, males sing less and spend their time warding off potential rivals. Females incubate their eggs and raise hatchlings with no help from males.

Although a male mates with all females nesting on his territory—sometimes as many as fifteen—there is no guarantee that all chicks from these nests are his. While he industriously attempts to chase away all intruders, including other males, hawks, and humans, females are doing a bit of philandering themselves. About twenty-five percent of the chicks from each nest are not sired by the male owner of that territory! Thus, both males and females opt to mate with a variety of individuals of the opposite sex.

Most bird species are monogamous and some even mate for life. In such species, males and females typically share chick-rearing duties because it often takes two to find enough food for hungry chicks. When food is plentiful, as it is on the breeding grounds of red-winged blackbirds, a species can be polygamous, with males focused on guarding their mates from male rivals and females in charge of parenting.

Although red-winged blackbirds today are abundant from Alaska to Central America, their choice of highly productive marshes for breeding could foreshadow a rapid population decline as wetlands are drained to make room for expanding human populations. If wetlands disappear, so might the seemingly ubiquitous red-winged blackbird.

32

DRAGONFLIES

Dragonflies are nimble denizens of the Mono Basin, inhabiting the lake's shorelines and other nearby aquatic habitats, such as the DeChambeau ponds. Dragonflies evolved over three hundred million years ago and were some of the first winged insects on earth. Early dragonflies were huge—some had two-foot wingspans—apparently the result of higher levels of oxygen at that time. The two-inch wingspans of dragonflies today, such as eight-spotted or flame skimmers, are a fraction of their former size.

Dragonflies perch on prominent vegetation, like reeds, to scan their environment for prey, competitors, or mates. Their excellent vision is made possible by huge eyes that account for almost their entire head. In flight they can hover like a helicopter, fly straight up or down, or zip forward, and skimmers get their name from their habit of flying low over water. While not strictly territorial, they aggressively chase off other dragonflies, regardless of species.

To mate, a male dragonfly grabs a female with his pincers in flight and drags her along behind him until she is willing to mate. After mating, he repels other potential suitors until the female finishes laying her eggs. Females dip their abdomens into the water and lay one egg at a time, in different locations, to ensure that nymphs don't cannibalize one another.

Nymphs (also called naiads, after female water nymphs in Greek mythology) are voracious eaters that consume mosquito larvae, tadpoles, and even small fish. Feeding nymphs shoot out pinchers to grab their prey and deliver it into their mouths, a completely different method than that used by adults. When a nymph reaches maturity, it crawls onto land where its exoskeleton cracks open. The adult dragonfly emerges and expands, much like a telescope. After its wings have stretched and dried, the new adult flies off, leaving behind its bizarre-looking nymphal skin.

Adult dragonflies are extremely efficient predators, catching prey in flight with their long legs. Dragonflies do humans a favor by consuming as many as one hundred mosquitoes per day, plus flies, no-see-ums (the bane of all summer travelers to the Mono Basin), and other soft-bodied insects. The flamboyant coloration of dragonflies and their aerial mating ballet make them an interesting group of insects for curious nature lovers to observe.

BUSHES, BUSHES, AND MORE BUSHES

The basin surrounding Mono Lake is a different world from the simple ecosystem driving the lake's productivity. The Mono Basin contains over 1,100 species of plants, most of them bushes, which provide cover and food for the animal inhabitants of the high Great Basin Desert. Only plants able to tolerate harsh conditions like a short growing season, extreme high and low temperatures, little rain, and thin volcanic soils can survive here.

The most salt-tolerant plants grow closest to the lake, as the soil nearest the lake is deeply infused with dried alkaline salts. Called "alkali sink scrub," this zone contains plants that have effective defense mechanisms to combat high salt content—glands that excrete salt, small narrow leaves, and waxy cuticles, all of which reduce water loss. The deep tap roots of these plants reach groundwater well beneath the surface, and their pale green leaves reflect sunlight.

Rubber rabbitbrush is perhaps the most salt-tolerant plant in the vicinity of Mono Lake, and its bright yellow blooms in late summer and early fall liven up the uniform gray-green of Mono Basin plant communities. Saltgrass

grows in mats near the lakeshore, and its blades are dotted with salt crystals at the points where salt is excreted. Caterpillar greasewood is another salt-tolerant plant found relatively close to the shoreline. It has a tap root as long as 129 feet and a root system whose tendrils extend to pools of groundwater.

Farther from the shore is sagebrush, the most dominant plant in the Mono Basin. Although not very salt-tolerant, sagebrush is well-adapted to thin volcanic soils, and like other plants in this zone, has a long tap root to access groundwater deep beneath the surface.

Farthest from shore is bitterbrush, the second most dominant bush in the region, and one of the least salt-tolerant plants native to the Mono Basin. Like other plants thriving in these thin, dry soils, it has a deep tap root. Bitterbrush can live to a ripe old age—the oldest known plant was 162 years old! Wildlife managers call bitterbrush "the ice cream plant" because its high protein content makes it a delicious and nutritious meal for mammals like mule deer.

What you won't find anywhere near the shoreline of Mono Lake, except perhaps where freshwater creeks empty into the lake, are trees. Trees in the Mono Basin, like pinyon pines and Utah junipers, thrive in the cooler temperatures and deeper, moister soils found at higher elevations.

PYGMY RABBIT

The diminutive pygmy rabbit is the most adorable of the approximately sixty species of leporids (rabbits and hares) in the world. Smallest in this group, pygmy rabbits are round balls of fluff with tails so inconspicuous that they are invisible, even when the animals are running away from you. The pygmy rabbit is easy to distinguish from the more common cottontail rabbit by its size and its ears, which are shorter, furrier, and more rounded than those of cottontails. We used to think that pygmy rabbits were closely related to cottontails, but now we believe that they represent a more primitive rabbit lineage that is only distantly related to cottontails.

Not only do pygmy rabbits prefer sagebrush habitat, they aren't found anywhere else. The diet of pygmy rabbits consists almost exclusively of sagebrush—up to ninety-nine percent in winter and about fifty percent in summer. Pygmy rabbits actually seem to prefer some sagebrush shrubs over others, which suggests that variation in plant chemistry and available nutrients influences their choice of forage. Mature sagebrush plants also provide shade and plenty of space underneath to hide from predators, and pygmy rabbits often spend a good part of their day nestled under this plant cover.

Unlike most other rabbits, pygmy rabbits construct burrows, which is why they inhabit areas with deep soft soils. The residential burrows they excavate beneath shrubs are three-to-six feet deep and have as many as eight entrances. Individual rabbits dig multiple burrows and move from one burrow to another. Generations of pygmy rabbits occupy the same burrow systems year after year.

Pygmy rabbits construct separate burrows for giving birth, which are shallower and have a terminal nest chamber lined with fur and vegetation. Like all rabbits, female pygmy rabbits are not doting mothers, returning to nurse their young only twice a day. After each nursing bout, mothers backfill their burrows with soil, essentially burying their babies to protect them from predators.

While pygmy rabbits are found in suitable sagebrush habitat across the Great Basin, the Mono Basin population, ranging from Bodie to Crowley Lake, is isolated and genetically distinct from rabbits in the core range of the species. Scientists believe that Mono Basin pygmy rabbits have been isolated for five-to-ten thousand years, similar to other sagebrush-dependent species in the Basin like greater sage grouse and dark kangaroo mice.

GREATER SAGE GROUSE

Walking along a dusty dirt road in the Mono Basin, a burst of noise and feathers explodes from the sagebrush. You have inadvertently "flushed" a group of greater sage grouse that was quietly munching on sagebrush leaves just a few feet away from you. After seeing that you are no threat to them, the grouse glide back to the ground and silently disappear into the sagebrush.

Greater sage grouse are polygamous—dominant males earn the privilege of mating with multiple females, while lower status males don't get to mate at all. The courtship displays of male greater sage grouse, designed to impress females, are so remarkable that human visitors gather to observe them each year. Males travel to their breeding "lek" to perform spectacular dances for females gathered round for the show. Lek is Nordic for "dance hall," and male greater sage grouse are renowned for their dancing; they puff out their chests, fill golden air sacs on their chests with huge gulps of air, thrust their heads this way and that, fan out their tails, and utter odd pops and whistles, all designed to win the favor of females. After careful observation, females select one or two of the males as most impressive and mate only with them. Males annually return to their leks to compete for females, so a different outcome is possible every year. Dancing and sperm are a male's only contributions to reproduction; after mating, females are on their own to parent solo.

Once called sage "chickens" because of their size and prolific numbers, populations of greater sage grouse have drastically declined in recent years. Their sagebrush habitat, on which they depend for food, shelter, and nesting sites, is threatened like never before. There are no protected sagebrush reserves in North America today, and most sagebrush habitat has been damaged or fragmented by livestock ranching, agriculture, gas and oil drilling, or mining. Highly flammable invasive grasses and climate change loom large as future threats to sagebrush ecosystems and increase the risk to this species, which cannot survive outside of this habitat.

Efforts to protect greater sage grouse are underway. Although several petitions to protect them under the Endangered Species Act have been denied, conservationists are gearing up to try again. And augmentation of Mono Basin populations of greater sage grouse has begun. Time will tell if the efforts to protect this remarkable species will ultimately prove successful.

GOPHER SNAKE

A three-to-eight foot long gopher snake can be a formidable sight, especially for someone who fears snakes. These sinuous yellow and brown serpents, however, are usually (but not always) docile and unaggressive to people, sometimes even when pestered. Edward Abbey tells a great story in *Desert Solitaire* about a large gopher snake he befriended in the hopes that it would repel a rattlesnake living beneath his trailer. He captured the gopher snake, let it loose in his trailer for a couple of weeks to "tame" it, and allowed it to wrap itself around his body, under his shirt, to keep warm. The gopher snake apparently didn't deter the rattlesnake, but it did rid Abbey's trailer of unwelcome four-legged visitors, like mice. Lest you think about stuffing a gopher snake under your shirt like Abbey did, know that they sometimes hiss and may even strike to protect themselves.

Gopher snakes are particularly adept at keeping rodent populations in check. They usually capture their preferred prey, like rodents and young rabbits, on land, but can climb trees to capture birds or swim to catch frogs. They move slowly, diligently investigating burrows and rocky crevices in search of their next meal. Gopher snakes are nonvenomous and kill by constriction.

Although gopher snakes are predators, they can just as easily become prey for red-tailed hawks, kit foxes, and coyotes. Sensing danger, a gopher snake protects itself by "pretending" to be a rattlesnake. It puffs up its body, flattens its head, coils up into the strike pose of a pit viper, and shakes its tail. The sound of a gopher snake's tail shaking in the leaf litter is easily mistaken for a rattle.

Gopher snakes inhabit all four deserts in the American Southwest, including the Great Basin Desert near Mono Lake, and camouflage themselves in vegetation. They hibernate in the winter like most snakes living in temperate climates, sometimes with other snake species.

When mating season arrives, the combat dances performed by males are thrilling to watch. Two males alternate gliding side by side, intertwining their bodies, and turning together in exquisite unison. An observer of this dance could easily wonder, as Abbey did, if it was part of an elaborate courtship ritual between the sexes, rather than a determinant of breeding rights.

LONG-TAILED WEASEL

Slinky. That one word best sums up the looks and behavior of the long-tailed weasel. These diminutive carnivores glide in and out of rocks when hunting for pikas, or slip effortlessly into burrows in pursuit of unsuspecting chipmunks or mice. They sneak up on prey often more than twice their size, jump onto their backs, and quickly pierce their skulls with their long, sharp canine teeth. Weasels are voracious predators which hunt day or night to meet their dietary needs. To add insult to injury, long-tailed weasels frequently move into the burrows of animals they have killed, lining their new digs with the fur of their victims.

Unlike most small mammals, long-tailed weasels are shaped like a long, narrow tube—a trait that allows them easy access to the burrows of their prey. Their physique, however, comes with a cost—increased heat loss. While most small mammals are rounder and can curl up in a ball to keep warm, weasels have more exposed surface area and shorter fur to insulate them from cold. To compensate for being long and thin, cold-stressed weasels must burn 50-100 percent more calories than other mammals of similar size. But the ability to efficiently hunt for prey more than compensates a weasel for the energetic cost of being slinky.

Long-tailed weasels are solitary, and as predators, there are fewer of them than the herbivorous small mammals they rely on for food. This can be a problem when males and females need to find one another during the breeding season. Weasels solve this dilemma by mating in late summer or early fall, when their population size is highest. When a female becomes pregnant, she delays the implantation of her fertilized embryos into her uterus for eight-to-nine months. As spring approaches, the embryos implant and develop normally. The birth of young weasels is thus exquisitely timed to when bountiful prey is most available, ensuring that mother weasels are able to successfully provision their litters.

Weasels are curious and inquisitive beasts. When encountering one in the field, feel free to approach it—just not too closely. The weasel initially may dart down a burrow or into the rocks, but it will soon reappear, standing erect, and gaze at you with great interest. One weasel I saw in the wild approached me, stood upright on the toe of my boot, and quizzically gave me the once over!

BEHR'S HAIRSTREAK BUTTERFLY

Whenever a new species is discovered in nature, it is described, named, and codified with a type specimen—an individual collected at that particular place. Such a specimen becomes the permanent reference for the new species. The type locality for Behr's hairstreak, discovered in 1870, is "Lake Mono." So while Behr's hairstreak occurs wherever bitterbrush grows across western North America, Mono Lake is its figurative home.

Behr's hairstreak butterflies are active in the Mono Basin from late June to early August, feeding on nectar from wildflowers like yarrow or buckwheat. Males perch conspicuously atop flowers or prominent shrubs where they scan for breeding females. Males typically keep their wings closed when perching and regulate their body temperature by orienting their wings toward or away from the sun.

Females avoid predation by choosing to be inconspicuous. In fact, the best way to see a female Behr's hairstreak is to shake a bitterbrush bush and see if any flutter out! Females emerge from their hiding places only to feed and then once again disappear into the foliage.

Females lay single eggs on antelope bitterbrush, as Behr's hairstreak caterpillars rely exclusively on this plant for food. Eggs lie dormant over winter and hatch into caterpillars the following spring, ready to voraciously consume bitterbrush leaves. Ants are common predators of many caterpillars, but some hairstreak species have evolved innovative defense mechanisms to foil attacks by ants. An ingenious defense found in one hairstreak species is the secretion of a honeydew-like substance which is so tantalizing to ants that they protect the caterpillar instead of eating it. The specific relationship between ants and Behr's hairstreak butterflies is still unknown.

In late spring, the caterpillar develops into a chrysalis, the third stage of the species' life cycle, and attaches itself to a bitterbrush stem. Two weeks later an adult Behr's hairstreak butterfly emerges, completing its life cycle.

Perhaps the most interesting fact about Behr's hairstreak butterflies in the Mono Basin is the huge fluctuation in their population size from year to year. In some years they are literally everywhere, but in other years they are extremely scarce. Migration can't explain these huge swings in population size because the Behr's hairstreak is not known to migrate. Even butterfly experts can't explain the unusual population dynamics of the Behr's hairstreak, leaving one more problem for the next generation of butterfly biologists to solve.

PRONGHORN

Pronghorns are the fastest land mammal in North America. They clock speeds approaching 60 mph, which undoubtedly allowed them to outrun their ancient predator, the extinct American cheetah. Their prominent black eyes are the largest of any hoofed animal, proportional to their size. Pronghorns are the only mammal with branched horns, and the only one that sheds its horns every year. The horns of a pronghorn have a permanent bony core and are covered by a black sheath of stiff hair-like material that grows back each summer after being shed in the fall.

Although often referred to as "pronghorn antelopes," pronghorns aren't antelopes. Surprisingly, they are most closely related to giraffes, and they are the only living member of a unique family of mammals that has lived in North America for over a million years. At one time our present-day pronghorns coexisted with three other species of pronghorn, all of which had four horns rather than two. The smallest of these pronghorn relatives stood a mere two feet tall.

Pronghorns are creatures of open country in western North America, where they once roamed in huge numbers—an estimated twenty-to-forty million in the early 1800s. Because of their abundance, pronghorns were a major food source for Native Americans, including the Kutzadika'a people, who have continuously inhabited the Mono Basin for millennia.

Hunting pronghorns was difficult because they could easily outrun their human predators. The Kutzadika'a solved this dilemma by building large funnel traps, because while pronghorns are fleet runners, they do not jump over barriers. Low walls made from juniper and sagebrush essentially confined the pronghorns so they could be chased into traps and killed with obsidian-tipped spears and arrows. Three funnel traps have been excavated within two and a half miles from the eastern shore of Mono Lake; the trap most recently discovered measured a half mile long, from its wings to the end of its corral. The Kutzadika'a used these traps to sustainably harvest pronghorn for 1400 years.

Conditions for pronghorns changed dramatically around 1860, as settlers moved into the Mono Basin and brought huge herds of sheep with them. By 1900, two hundred thousand sheep were mowing down native grasses in the Mono Basin. The diverse, lush, green vegetation east of Mono Lake was devoured by these "hoofed locusts," a term aptly coined by John Muir. With nothing left to eat, the pronghorn population east of Mono Lake disappeared, never to return.

A ray of hope, however, remains for pronghorns in the Mono Basin. One population now resides in the Bodie Hills, north of Mono Lake, resulting from the reintroduction of thirty-two animals there from 1946 to 1947. There are now approximately 150 animals in this migratory herd, which spends winters in Nevada and summers in California. These pronghorns approach the lower Mono Basin via Black Point, the southern slopes of Mt. Biedeman, or DeChambeau Ranch. Although some say this population is stable, others believe that grazing, fencing, poaching, mining, and climate change continue to pose serious threats to this very special herd. Only time will tell.

GREAT BASIN SPADEFOOT

The Great Basin spadefoot "toad" isn't really a toad—it is actually a member of a unique family of amphibians whose only members are other spadefoot species. Spadefoots get their name from the glossy, black, sharp-edged "spade" on each hind foot. This appendage allows a spadefoot to dig a burrow up to three feet deep in which it shelters during its long winter period of inactivity. Great Basin spadefoots spend nearly all winter underground, doing essentially nothing beyond maintaining their metabolism and readying themselves for reproduction. During these lengthy inactive periods, spadefoots lose up to forty-eight percent of their body moisture, without apparent ill effect.

In summer, spadefoots rise to the surface when conditions for breeding are optimal—warm temperatures plus a soaking rainstorm. When spadefoots become surface active, however, they enter the eat-or-be-eaten world. They mainly eat ants and other insects, and in turn, are eaten by rattlesnakes, coyotes, and burrowing owls. Spadefoots have two main strategies to avoid becoming a predator's next meal. First, camouflaging coloration makes them nearly indistinguishable from rocks when sitting still. If their camouflage fails, they can emit foul-smelling skin secretions that may encourage predators to search for less disgusting prey.

Great Basin spadefoots thrive in sagebrush flats in loose, sandy soils, in which they can easily dig a new burrow or opportunistically commandeer one that is currently unoccupied. When it is time to breed, spadefoots must travel to springs or other permanent water sources. Huge numbers of spadefoots hopping along on their way to their breeding grounds is both a spectacular sight and a road hazard for unsuspecting drivers who suddenly encounter hundreds of them crossing the road. We don't know how far spadefoots travel, but estimates vary from a half mile to several miles.

Once on their breeding grounds, males chorus loudly to attract females to mate with them. Females lay up to a thousand eggs in the water, in packets of twenty-to-forty eggs. Eggs hatch in two-to-four days, and tadpoles grow for almost fifty more days before their forelimbs develop. During this time tadpoles feed on algae, invertebrates, carrion, and carcasses of dead tadpoles, and they are preyed upon by garter snakes and egrets. After metamorphosis is complete, young spadefoots live on land, returning to water only to breed. They reach their adult size at age three and live for up to ten years.

DARK KANGAROO MOUSE

All organisms have an official two-word name (genus and species) in Latin. These names are often as hard to pronounce as they are to remember, which is why you won't find them in most of our accounts. We make an exception for the dark kangaroo mouse because its scientific name is exquisitely apt. The genus is *Microdipodops* (micro = small; dipodops = kangaroo rat), and the species is *megacephalus* (mega = large; cephalus = head). The dark kangaroo mouse is thus a smaller version of the better-known kangaroo rat—with a giant head.

Dark kangaroo mice hop along on their huge hind feet like kangaroos. Their small front legs and feet perform like a powerful vacuum cleaner, filtering sand from seeds. The mice then pack the seeds into their external, fur-lined cheek pouches until ready to store them in their underground burrows. Dark kangaroo mice also have excellent peripheral vision, thanks to their large eyes, which improves their detection of predators while they are out foraging.

Kangaroo mice are active from spring through fall and spend the winter in nests they build deep in their burrows. Because the abundance of seeds, their main source of food, is highly variable, dark kangaroo mice must rely on a variety of strategies to survive the winter. First, they draw upon their cache of seeds. When seed stores are limited, the mice become torpid—they lower their body temperature to reduce energetic costs. Finally, the ability of kangaroo mice to store fat in their tails provides an extra source of energy to help get them through the winter. The very fat tails characteristic of these mice in the fall are slender once again when the mice emerge in the spring.

Sandy soils, generally in sagebrush scrub or alkali sink plant communities, are characteristic of kangaroo mouse habitat. While kangaroo mice are found in this type of habitat throughout the Great Basin, their distribution in the Mono Basin is isolated from the species' primary geographic range, similar to the greater sage grouse and pygmy rabbit. These three species are found only in sagebrush habitat, perhaps because they responded similarly to climate change during the late Pleistocene and early Holocene, thousands of years ago. The numbers of all three species are threatened today because their sagebrush habitat is becoming fragmented or even eliminated by the expansion of pinyon pines, increase in wildfires, competition from invasive grasses, and cattle grazing.

LOGGERHEAD SHRIKE

The black-masked loggerhead shrike, with its velvety gray back, black wings, and white throat, spends eighty percent of its time sitting quietly on a high perch, waiting for a tasty prey item to fly or amble by. In an instant, the shrike dive-bombs its prey, decapitating it or breaking its neck with its sharply-pointed hooked bill. Tufa towers at Mono Lake are excellent perches for a shrike scanning for its next meal.

"Butcherbird" is an apt nickname for this small predator, unique among songbirds for its carnivorous diet. Because loggerhead shrikes have the delicate feet of songbirds, rather than talons, they can't hold their prey and eat at the same time, like a hawk or an owl. To solve this problem, a shrike skewers its dead prey, be it reptile, bird, or mammal, onto the nearest available spike, thorn, or barbed-wire fence. The shrike can then choose to consume its prey now or later, as it pleases. Large insects are also a favorite food, but are typically consumed when captured in flight.

Having a larder of dead prey hanging from various hooks is not only convenient for a loggerhead shrike when hungry, especially during winter, but may also increase a male's attractiveness to females during the breeding season. Females skewer prey less frequently than males do, so a display of luscious rotting prey on a male's territory may be hard for a female to resist.

Loggerhead males have a number of ways to attract females during the breeding season, like performing aerial dances or offering them food, a behavior called "courtship feeding." After mating, females build their nests, lay their eggs, and incubate them, all without any help from their mates. But both males and females actively feed the chicks, in the nest or out of it, until the young learn to hunt on their own. Unfortunately, many newly hatched chicks don't survive, and dead youngsters are efficiently gobbled up by their parents or fed to their surviving siblings.

Although still common in western North America, the number of loggerhead shrikes has declined in recent years, and this species is now labeled "near threatened" by the U.S. Fish and Wildlife Service. Ranging from Canada to northern Mexico, populations of loggerhead shrikes began to decline in the mid-1900s, due to consumption of insect prey laden with pesticides. The biggest threat to loggerhead shrikes today is loss of habitat.

GIANT BLAZINGSTAR

If you are exploring the northern shore of Mono Lake in midsummer, you might be lucky enough to see hundreds of sun-loving giant blazingstars, which are biennial or short-lived perennial wildflowers that thrive in the sandy, well-drained soils of the Mono Basin. Each plant may be up to three feet tall and is covered with a profusion of huge, star-shaped yellow flowers. In between five pointed petals are long thin yellow sepals, and the blazingstar's center is literally bursting with whiskery yellow stamens. The flowers open at dusk and close in early afternoon, so they can be pollinated day or night.

Like much of the vegetation in the Mono Basin, the blazingstar's leaves are a pale sage green, to better reflect light and conserve water. Buds are elongated and are the color of frothy peach gelato. If you brush past a blazingstar, you might discover that its leaves have adhered to your clothing, giving rise to the blazingstar's nickname—"nature's velcro."

Giant blazingstars produce seeds that some northern Paiute tribes historically used for food and medicine. Seeds were ground into flour and then made into a mush. The roots of blazingstars were used by native peoples to treat an impressive array of ailments, including rheumatism, earaches, measles, and small pox.

Thick with pollen and nectar, giant blazingstars attract native bees, butterflies, hawk moths, and other moth species. A particularly interesting visitor to these flowers is the white-lined sphinx moth, which upon first sight is often mistaken for a hummingbird. Nearly the size of hummingbirds, the foraging behavior of the white-lined sphinx moth—hovering in front of flowers and flapping its wings while feeding—closely resembles that of hummingbirds. Because sphinx moth caterpillars rear their heads up in alarm when they sense danger, sphinx moths were named for the resemblance of their caterpillars to Egyptian sphinxes.

White-lined sphinx moths belong to the hawk moth family and are abundant across North America. Acute eyesight and a keen sense of smell help sphinx moths find nectar, their preferred food. When sphinx moths feed on blazingstars, their chocolate and cream-colored stripes are a striking contrast to the bright yellow flowers, producing a welcome splash of color in a sea of gray and sage green.

AMERICAN PIKA

Most American pikas in California live on rocky slopes, called talus, adjacent to verdant alpine meadows high in the Sierra Nevada. Astute pika observers will cry "foul" upon seeing an account of pikas in a book about the Mono Basin. But tell that to the pikas who live in the Mono Craters, a mere two miles from the shoreline of Mono Lake.

The discovery of pikas in the Mono Craters is perplexing—like finding pikas on the moon. How did they get there and how similar is their ecology to that of pikas living in the nearby High Sierra? One common feature of all pikas is that they are relatively sedentary and unlikely to disperse across even moderate distances. We believe that pikas colonized the craters from the Sierra during an earlier, colder period that was more conducive to pika dispersal.

Pikas are strict herbivores and they don't hibernate. During summer pikas must cache enough vegetation in "haypiles" to allow them to survive the winter, when snow blankets their food supply. Males and females defend individual, adjoining, territories on their talus habitat, and they are primarily active during the day. Pikas are highly vocal, advertising their territory with short calls ("eh-eh") or a long call, uttered only by males during the breeding season.

Pikas in the Mono Craters follow most of this playbook, but with a few twists. They utter vocalizations at about the same rate as Sierra pikas, but their overall activity level is far lower than their Sierra cohorts. And vegetation growing near talus in the Mono Craters is far less abundant than that found in the High Sierra. As a result, Mono Craters pikas defend larger territories than Sierra pikas and don't always construct a traditional haypile; some simply scatter smaller caches of vegetation across their territory.

Pikas are very sensitive to warm temperatures, and the Mono Craters are far hotter than one would expect for a pika-occupied site. Pikas avoid the hottest temperatures by being active primarily in the early morning or late afternoon, and sometimes, even at night. But one feature of the Mono Craters environment contributes to the ability of pikas to withstand hot surface temperatures—the presence of a lens of permafrost beneath the surface. This ancient structure was made possible by the unique porosity of the rhyolite sand and pumice that formed the craters. Placing your hand inside one of the openings that pikas dart in and out of during the day, you will feel a cold blast of air—the pikas' very own private air conditioner.

RIPARIAN COMMUNITIES

Plant communities lining streams and riverbanks, called "riparian zones," are ribbons of green snaking across an arid landscape that provide some of the most valuable habitat in the southwestern U.S. Their role in maintaining the Mono Basin ecosystem is huge. First, five major streams flowing out of the Sierra Nevada transport nearly all the fresh water that replenishes Mono Lake. Second, riparian areas winding through sagebrush communities are nutrient-rich ecosystems with unique soil characteristics that support far more plant and animal species than adjacent upland areas—many species even migrate there to breed. Third, riparian zones reduce downstream flooding and regenerate groundwater. And fourth, the winding pathways of riparian communities provide a corridor in which dispersing or migrating animals are better concealed from predators while on the move.

Rush Creek is the largest stream in the Mono Basin (forty-one percent of the total runoff), followed by Lee Vining Creek (thirty-three percent), Mill Creek (fourteen percent), Parker Creek (six percent), and Walker Creek (four percent). The riparian zones associated with these creeks originally were lined with almost continuous forest habitat—Jeffrey pines, cottonwoods, aspens, willows—to within a short distance of Mono Lake. The lush vegetation hugging these stream banks supported thousands of ducks and other wildlife species. Channels in Rush and Lee Vining Creeks also offered good spawning habitat for trout.

In the early 1900s all of these streams were tamed to provide hydropower and irrigation for agriculture. Peak flows of Rush Creek were greatly reduced by three dams built in its headwaters to form Waugh, Gem, and Agnew Lakes. Similarly, dams enlarging Saddlebag, Tioga, and Ellery Lakes in the Sierra greatly reduced the maximum peak flow of Lee Vining Creek. A dam enlarging Grant Lake and smaller diversion structures on Parker and Walker Creeks diverted water for agricultural irrigation. Another dam enlarged Lundy Lake to provide hydropower, and additional structures captured Mill Creek water to irrigate local pastures.

In spite of these alterations to the feeder creeks emptying into Mono Lake, all continued to flow and support healthy riparian communities until 1941. Large pines and cottonwoods thrived near the lakeshore, and these streambank ecosystems continued to provide important habitat for native wildlife.

And then the city of Los Angeles got thirsty.

QUAKING ASPEN

If you ask visitors to Mono County what they find special about quaking aspen, they might mention the tree's dazzling fall color, ranging from gold to salmon pink. Or they might say that, with just the slightest breeze, an aspen's heart-shaped leaves "tremble almost incessantly, like thousands of fluttering butterfly wings." This "quaking" occurs because of the long flat petioles that are attached at a ninety-degree angle to an aspen's flat leaves. But aspens are more than just another gorgeous tree in the forest—their natural history is extraordinary.

What appears to be an individual aspen tree is instead part of a far larger organism. A clone of multiple trunks connected through a vast shared underground root system allows individual trees to share nutrients or water via their common root system. All trees within a clone are both genetically identical and the same sex. After losing their leaves in the winter, like all deciduous trees, aspens in the same clone leaf out in unison in the spring, providing an easy way to accurately identify the boundaries of each clone.

Aspens usually reproduce asexually by sending out root sprouts. Sexual reproduction is far more rare because multiple obstacles reduce its chance of success. First, seeds are produced when eggs on female clones are wind-pollinated by pollen from male clones. The resulting huge numbers of tiny seeds (up to two million per pound) then must be dispersed by the wind, sometimes over great distances. Because aspen seeds have neither a protective coat nor a stored food source, few survive long enough to germinate. But on the infrequent occasions when all of these obstacles are overcome, a new aspen seedling sprouts and eventually gives rise to a new, genetically different clone.

Aspen trees provide "ecosystem services" to a variety of wildlife species. Their striking white bark carries out photosynthesis throughout the winter, which both increases the tree's overwinter survival and provides an important source of food for cottontail rabbits, deer, and birds when other types of trees are dormant. Hole-nesting birds often choose an aspen for nesting because its soft wood is easy to excavate.

Here are some remarkable records held by aspen trees. Aspens are the most widely distributed tree in North America, and some are even older than sequoias or bristlecone pines. One aspen clone in Utah, named "Pando," is the largest and heaviest living organism on Earth, covering 106 acres and weighing over thirteen million pounds!

RED-BREASTED SAPSUCKER

In April or May in the Mono Basin, it seems like red-breasted sapsuckers are everywhere. Unmistakable with their bright red heads, pale yellow bellies, and black and white zebra-striped backs, these medium-sized woodpeckers migrate here to breed in aspen and cottonwood trees.

What is the difference between a woodpecker and a sapsucker, you might ask? It's all about the holes they drill. Woodpeckers drill larger holes, anywhere on a tree, while sapsuckers drill small, neat holes, typically in horizontal rows. Sapsuckers visit and revisit the holes to check for newly flowing sugary sap, their primary source of food, and have a brush-like tongue perfectly designed to lap it up. On rare occasions, sapsuckers have actually killed a tree with their overzealous drilling.

Red-breasted sapsuckers may or may not be aware that they have stalkers. Tiny rufous hummingbirds, which also migrate to the Mono Basin to breed, follow sapsuckers from hole to hole to feast on any leftover sap. Red-breasted sapsuckers are actually considered to be a "keystone" species (a species on which other species in an ecosystem depend) because other species, like the rufous hummingbird, make use of the sap wells they drill.

It is no surprise that a bird whose head and strong beak can withstand constant drumming on trees also gouges out cavities in trees for nesting. Red-breasted sapsuckers are monogamous, and each year a breeding pair excavates a new nest hole, rather than return to an old one. Both parents feed the nestlings and then spend about ten days teaching their fledglings how to forage for sap and insects before leaving them to fend for themselves. A pair of red-breasted sapsuckers raises only one brood per season.

While sapsuckers specialize in foraging for sap, like all woodpeckers, they also glean insects from tree bark or nab them in flight, and take advantage of seasonal berries. They are easily identified as a woodpecker in flight by their classic "flap flap glide" pattern of wing beats. Like most woodpeckers, sapsuckers have two toes facing forward and two facing backward to more easily grasp and move around on tree trunks, their preferred perches.

PANAMINT ALLIGATOR LIZARD

Alligator lizards get their name from the shape of their head and body and from their belly scales, reinforced by bone, which are similar to those characteristic of alligators. The widespread northern and southern alligator lizards preferentially inhabit forests and woodlands, and often cohabit with humans by infiltrating their backyards or garages.

Not so for the Panamint alligator lizard, found only in Inyo and Mono Counties in California, which avoids humans and inhabits isolated riparian areas punctuated by rock piles, or talus. It is a secretive hunter of small invertebrates, bird eggs, or young birds still confined to their nests. Sometimes it waits for prey to appear, and sometimes it actively searches for food. It spends its days hiding or foraging in densely vegetated rocky canyons near streams or natural springs.

Alligator lizards are like other reptiles in that they must use their behavior (basking in the sun) or a refuge (a cool, shady spot) to regulate their body temperature. But unlike most other reptiles, alligator lizards can dart away from or avoid detection by a predator even before they are thoroughly warmed up—an extraordinarily handy trait for a reptile.

Panamint alligator lizards are prey choices for many snake species like California kingsnakes and Panamint rattlesnakes. But alligator lizards have effective strategies to escape from predators. Their first response is to quickly climb away from them or drop to the ground. When nabbed by a predator, they may bite or defecate on it, or even play dead, to avoid being eaten. They often distract predators by amputating their own tails, a less drastic strategy than one might think, as the tail eventually grows back to its original color and form.

Although Panamint alligator lizards are found only in California, they are actually more closely related to alligator lizards native to deserts, like those found in Arizona. It is difficult to assess their conservation status because they are so rarely seen—most of their range is remote, and sixty-five percent of the lands they inhabit are designated as wilderness. Although some of their habitat is threatened by mining, livestock grazing, and off-road vehicles, the greatest threat to these lizards undoubtedly is climate change. As seeps and springs dry up and surface water decreases, these denizens of riparian habitats will find less vegetation to hide in and fewer insects to eat.

WHERE ARE ALL THE DUCKS?

Before 1941, around one million migrating ducks touched down on Mono Lake every September. The sky was literally black with ducks every fall, as birds arrived to fatten up for their southern migration. Flotillas of ducks gathered in stream deltas and brackish lagoons where fresh water from creeks or springs emptied into Mono Lake. Although ducks don't tolerate salt well, they could drift along on the layer of fresh water floating atop the salty lake water. After diving into the saline depths to gobble up brine shrimp or alkali flies, they surfaced, rinsing off their feathers in fresh water. Northern shovelers feasted on brine shrimp, while mallards, green-winged teal, American widgeons, and gadwalls preferred alkali flies. Lake-fringing wetlands provided another source of food for ducks. Today fewer than fifteen thousand ducks visit Mono Lake on their way to their wintering or breeding grounds. What happened?

The population of Los Angeles was skyrocketing. To meet the city's water demands, the Los Angeles Department of Water and Power (LADWP) purchased land across the Mono Basin to gain control over the streams flowing into Mono Lake. An aqueduct system was built to send water from the mountains directly to Los Angeles, bypassing Mono Lake. Deprived of nearly all sources of water, Mono Lake began to shrink and became even saltier.

The diversion of water from Rush, Parker, Walker, and Lee Vining Creeks was absolute; their downstream riparian areas were deprived of all their water. Abutting marshes, ponds, and wetlands dried up and 260 acres of brackish lagoons disappeared. Riparian vegetation, like pine and cottonwood trees, perished. Sandy beaches became sticky mud flats. The water level in Mono Lake dropped precipitously.

By 1957, the habitats favored by ducks were essentially gone. Increasing salinity in Mono Lake decreased the productivity of brine shrimp and alkali flies. There was no longer enough food or adequate habitat to support a million migrating ducks.

So, most of the ducks disappeared. Ruddy ducks were the only exception, perhaps because they tolerate salt water better than other ducks, and they continue to stop at Mono Lake on their way south.

Can the lake and riparian communities be restored to levels that would once again attract ducks? In the 1990s, the courts ordered LADWP to restore the creeks and waterfowl habitats that were destroyed during the years of maximum diversion, but for many years, LADWP employed every delay tactic imaginable. Today, however, the stream restoration plan has been implemented and the streams are on the road to recovery.

SAVING MONO LAKE

Mono Lake was nearly destroyed. If it hadn't been for a band of intrepid undergraduate students, environmental organizations like the Mono Lake Committee, the Audubon Society, Friends of the Earth, and CalTrout, plus a few attorneys working pro bono and a sympathetic judge here and there, Mono Lake would have become just another dried up salt lake. Although snowmelt runoff from the High Sierra provided enough water to keep Mono Lake healthy, that water would not empty into the lake today had it not been for the intervention of hundreds of activists over the last fifty years.

The fight to save Mono Lake began in 1978, but threats to the lake were already looming in the early 1900s, when the city of Los Angeles discovered it lacked enough fresh water to accommodate its rapidly growing population. The solution? The Los Angeles Department of Water and Power (LADWP) would first buy up land in the Owens Valley and then in the Mono Basin, take control of the streams and rivers that emptied into Owens and Mono Lakes, and send the water via aqueduct to Los Angeles.

For a mere five million dollars, LADWP purchased the rights to thirty thousand acres of land in the Mono Basin, and additional water rights and easements on thousands more. The first stream to be diverted was Lee Vining Creek, followed by Rush Creek and its two tributaries, Parker and Walker Creeks. By 1941, Rush Creek, once a great trout fishing stream, ran dry for the first time.

Mono Lake shrunk in size with every passing year. As the lake level dropped, tufa began protruding above its surface, creating the skyline of tufa towers Mono Lake is famous for today. The declining lake level also exposed more of the salt playa. On windy days, thick dust storms of toxic chemicals obliterated the view of the lake and irritated the lungs of anyone unfortunate enough to be within breathing distance. Local people began organizing to protect the lake by forming "Friends of Mono Lake." The National Audubon Society and the Sierra Club also began to weigh in, but none of these early attempts to bring attention to the plight of Mono Lake were successful.

The general public first became acutely aware that Mono Lake was shrinking in 1977, when a land bridge to Negit Island emerged, allowing coyotes easy access to the island. The coyotes plundered the breeding colony of California gulls, the third largest in the world, gorging on chicks and eggs.

In the mid-1970s a group of undergraduate science students attending Stanford University and UC Davis received a grant to survey the birds of Mono Lake. Camping near the northwest corner of the lake and working on a shoestring budget, the students counted huge numbers of shorebirds whose primary food sources were the trillions of brine shrimp and alkali flies   living in the lake. The students understood that the health of brine shrimp and alkali flies would determine the number of birds on the lake, so they tried to pin down the highest salinity that these microorganisms could tolerate. Subsequent researchers came up with the answer: when Mono Lake dropped to 6350 feet, the increased salinity would kill all of its microorganisms, resulting in the ecosystem's collapse. Preventing this outcome looked impossible, however, given that LADWP had been granted a permanent license to take ALL the water from feeder streams in 1974.

Naturalist David Gaines and one of the student researchers formed the Mono Lake Committee in 1978 to try to save Mono Lake. Gaines spent most of the next two years presenting a slide show about Mono Lake to every group that invited him. Although people were learning more about Mono Lake from spectacular photographs of tufa groves and articles in magazines like *Outside*, *Smithsonian*, and *National Geographic*, the lake continued to shrink.

The Mono Lake Committee then enlisted another wave of activists. As an undergraduate student at UC Berkeley, Tim Such had pondered using the "Public Trust Doctrine" to fight LADWP, but found no one willing to help him pursue that strategy. The essence of this ancient doctrine is that public lands and bodies of water belong to all people, and the government must play the role of guardian and protect them. In 1978, Such persuaded a law firm to take the case pro bono, with a minimum of financial support from the Audubon Society, the Mono Lake Committee, and Friends of the Earth. The case took many turns, but finally was heard by the California Supreme Court. The court ruled in 1983 that the Public Trust Doctrine could be applied to Mono Lake, but didn't dictate how or when LADWP should stop diverting the water. So the diversion continued.

In the end, Mono Lake was saved by some non-native German brown trout stocked in mountain lakes and streams for sport fishing. In two high-water years, a few brown and rainbow trout were swept over two local dams—one year into Rush Creek and another year into Lee Vining Creek. A little known and basically ignored Fish & Game code enacted in the late 1800s protected any fish "planted or existing" below a dam. The Public Trust Doctrine was applied to Rush and Lee Vining Creeks, and after several studies showed that trout were indeed swimming in both creeks, a judge ruled that both creeks must be allowed to continue to flow! In 1988, the California Third District Court of Appeals ruled that the diversion of water had been illegal and the permanent license for LADWP to divert water from Rush and Lee Vining Creeks was amended. LADWP continues to divert some water, but most of the Mono Basin's fresh water now flows into Mono Lake.

Thus hundreds of human advocates, with the help of a few trout, saved the Mono Lake ecosystem. In 1994 the California State Water Resources Control Board ordered that Mono Lake must rise to 6392 feet—a level low enough to prevent the famous tufa towers from once again disappearing under the lake's surface, but high enough to keep the creeks flowing and Mono Lake's algae, brine shrimp, and alkali flies healthy and reproducing. It was assumed that Mono Lake would reach the prescribed level in about twenty years, but as of 2021, twenty-seven years later, the lake hovers at an elevation of around 6381 feet, still eleven feet short of the goal.

So, the saga of saving Mono Lake continues. But the eco-warriors that saved the lake—student researchers, David Gaines and the Mono Lake Committee, several environmental NGOs, Tim Such, lawyers willing to work pro bono, the California courts, and of course, the trout—all played essential roles in preserving the magnificent, majestic Mono Lake.

INVASIVE SPECIES

Another serious threat to the Mono Lake ecosystem, and a leading cause of the loss of biodiversity worldwide, is the spread of invasive animal or plant species. Invasive plants are non-native species that cause ecological or economic harm in their new environment because they outcompete native plants for nutrients and space to grow.

Developing the capacity to address the spread of invasive plants emerged during the fight for Mono Lake's water rights, and employees of the Inyo National Forest, Mono Lake Tufa State Natural Reserve, the Mono Lake Committee, California State Parks, Point Blue Conservation Science, and hundreds of volunteers have tackled the insidious spread of invasive plants in the Mono Basin.

For over a decade, non-native white sweet clover has been removed from the lower reaches of Mill Creek and from the Mono Lake Tufa State Natural Reserve. This clover grows five feet high and produces easily dispersed light seeds that can remain viable for up to thirty years. Removing this invasive species allows native plants to thrive and enhances restoration efforts on Mill Creek.

Don't be misled by the beautiful pink flowers of the invasive tamarisk, also known as saltcedar, a small tree native to Central Asia. Tamarisk spreads rapidly and has damaged riparian ecosystems across the American West. This thirsty plant increases fire frequency, changes streambed hydrology, lowers water tables, and increases soil salinity in riparian habitats. The first Mono Basin tamarisk was discovered at South Tufa in the 1980s. A GPS program was developed that predicts where tamarisk is likely to thrive, allowing removal of young plants before they take hold. Although the eradication of tamarisk in the Mono Basin has been wildly successful, continued vigilance is required because this highly invasive plant could suddenly reappear at any time.

California gulls, which nest on rocky ground on Mono Lake islets, face the threat of another invasive plant—the five-horn smotherweed. The branches of this tall plant densely cover the ground, preventing gulls from nesting. Smotherweed has covered more than seventy percent of the gulls' nesting grounds, which caused a precipitous decline in the number of chicks. Volunteers and conservationists worked together to remove this noxious weed from Twain Islet in spring 2020, using a combination of burning and manual clearing. Preliminary results from the 2020 breeding season were promising—there were over three thousand more nests than the year before. Collaborations like these are crucial for discovering and quickly eradicating the next generation of invasive plants.

CLIMATE CHANGE

The previous two chapters demonstrate how the energy and determination of people, applied to a common cause, can reverse the trajectory of environmental degradation at the local level. What hundreds of scientists, conservationists, attorneys, and nature lovers have done to save Mono Lake is awe-inspiring. But the existential threat of climate change is beyond what can be accomplished at the local level—it will take all of us pulling together to ensure that our planet remains livable.

Increasing temperatures will increase the evaporation rate from Mono Lake. The chemical balance of the lake will then change, and the resulting increases in salinity and alkalinity will endanger the lives of the microorganisms that drive the ecosystem. Changing patterns of precipitation are likely to decrease rainfall, which will reduce input to Mono Lake from its five feeder streams. Drought and/or higher temperatures will stress native plants, opening the door to invasive species, which could alter today's ecosystem beyond recognition.

As the lake level declines, more and more tufa will be exposed, and once tufa is exposed, it dies. Ghostly towers, crumbling in the heat, on a lakebed without water, is what the future may portend.

In this little book we have shared our fascination with and love of the beauty and resilience of the magnificent, majestic Mono Lake. We hope it inspires your love of nature and your determination to do all you can to protect Mono Lake, and our beautiful planet Earth, from irreversible change and destruction. The threat of climate change cannot be brushed aside. It is up to all of us to preserve Mono Lake and the world we live in.

FURTHER READING

Bowker, Davin, Cheryl Ecklund, and Michelle Hofmann. 2015. South Tufa: a Self-Guided Walking Tour. Kutsavi Press: Lee Vining, California.

Constantine, Helen. 1993. Plant Communities of the Mono Basin. Kutsavi Press: Lee Vining, California.

Hart, John. 1996. Storm over Mono. University of California Press: Berkeley and Los Angeles, California.

Hill, Mary. 2006. Geology of the Sierra Nevada. University of California Press: Berkeley and Los Angeles, California.

Mono Lake Newsletter. Mono Lake Committee. [all issues are archived at: https://www.monolake.org/learn/newsletter/]

Tierney, Tim. 2014. Geology of the Mono Basin. Kutsavi Press: Lee Vining, California.

ACKNOWLEDGEMENTS

We would like to thank Elin Ljung, Arya Harp, Bartshe Miller, and Nora Livingston for their careful review of all chapters pertaining to Mono Lake, its ecosystem, and its surrounding plant communities. Thomas Gill reviewed the chapter on the deadly beach. We are indebted to David Pearson for reviewing all chapters about birds. Constance Millar reviewed the chapters on riparian communities, aspen trees, and pronghorn. The chapter on dragonflies was reviewed by Pierre Deviche, and Phil McNally and Ron Rutowski reviewed the chapter on Behr's hairstreak butterfly. Dale DeNardo and J. Rachel Smith reviewed the chapters on gopher snakes and Panamint alligator lizards, and James Collins reviewed the chapter on spadefoots. Small mammal chapters were reviewed by John Harris. David Marquart provided reference materials for the chapters on ducks and saving Mono Lake, as well as invaluable suggestions about which plant and animal species to choose for focused species accounts. Most of all, we want to thank the Mono Lake Committee for its valiant, unremitting efforts for over fifty years to save the magnificent, majestic Mono Lake.

CPSIA information can be obtained
at www.ICGtesting.com
Printed in the USA
LVHW070834090622
720761LV00009B/434

9 781954 000308